throughout all generations, forever and ever. Amen.

—Ephesians 3:21

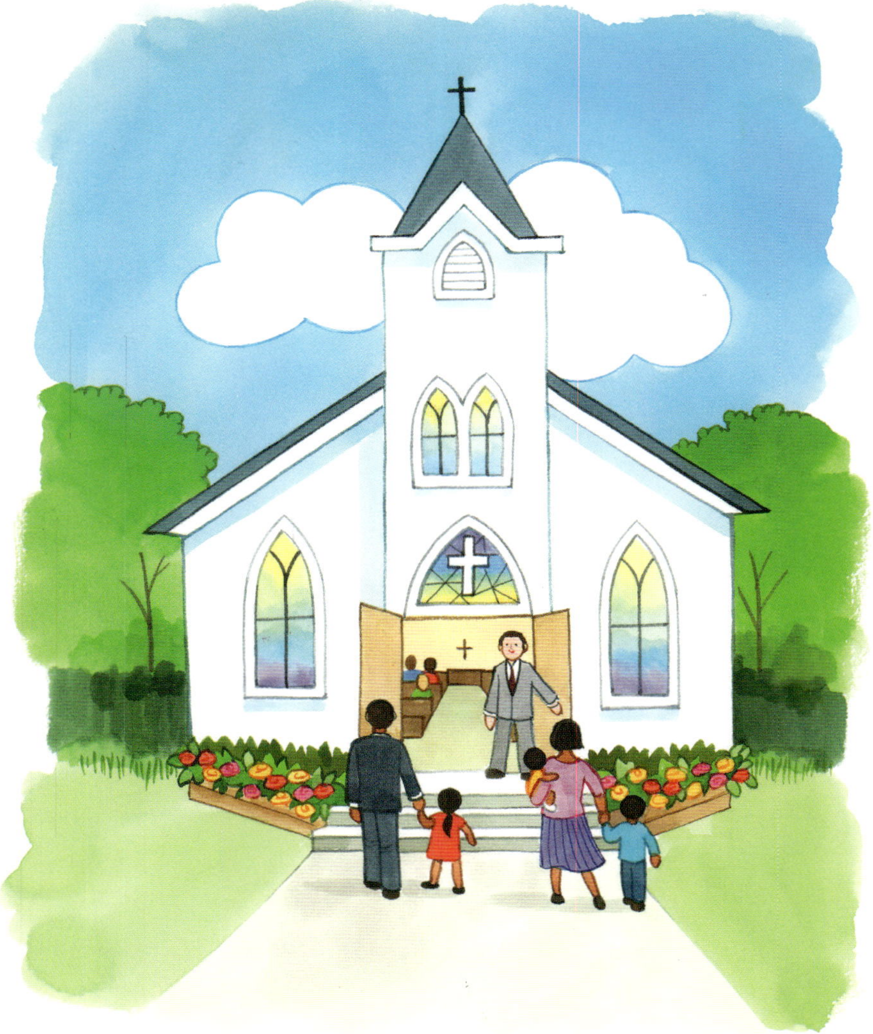

SCHEELE MEMORIAL LIBRARY

3 6655 00123065 4

JUV BOARD BOOK STOHLS ANITA
Stohls, Anita Reith
Here is the church

Curriculum Materials Center

**Concordia College Library
Bronxville, NY 10708**

Published by Concordia Publishing House
3558 S. Jefferson Ave.
St. Louis, MO 63118-3968
1-800-325-3040 • www.cph.org

Text © 2008 by Anita Reith Stohs
Illustrations © 2008 Concordia Publishing House
All rights reserved. No part of this publication may be reproduced, stored in a retrieval system, or transmitted, in any form or by any means, electronic, mechanical, photocopying, recording, or otherwise, without the prior written permission of Concordia Publishing House.

Scripture quotations, unless otherwise noted, are from the Holy Bible, English Standard Version ®. Copyright © 2001 by Crossway Bibles, a publishing ministry of Good News Publishers, Wheaton, Illinois. Used by permission. All rights reserved.

Manufactured in China
1 2 3 4 5 6 7 8 9 10
17 16 15 14 13 12 11 10 09 08

Here Is the Church

Anita Reith Stohs
Illustrated by Kathy Mitter

CONCORDIA PUBLISHING HOUSE • SAINT LOUIS

Here is the church, and

Here is the steeple,

Open the door to

See all God's people.

Action: *Fold hands with the fingers on the inside; put up index fingers to make a steeple. Open hands to show fingers.*

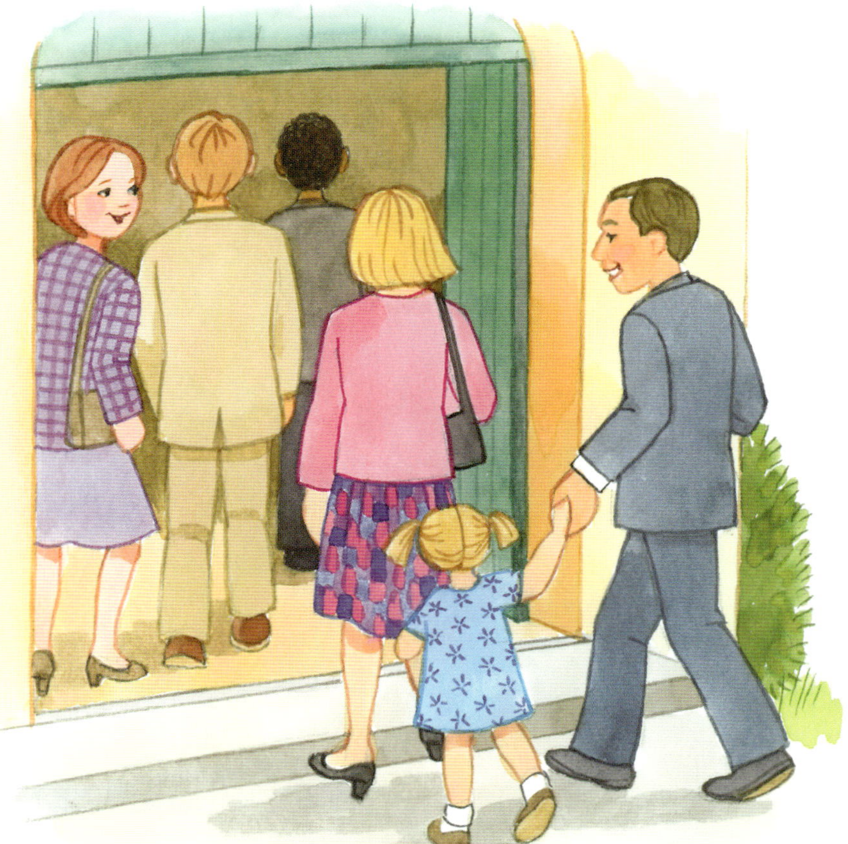

Now in a pew,
Fold hands to pray.
Ask God to bless
Your worship today.

Action: *Fold hands in prayer; point to heaven for "God." Or just use prayer hand motion.*

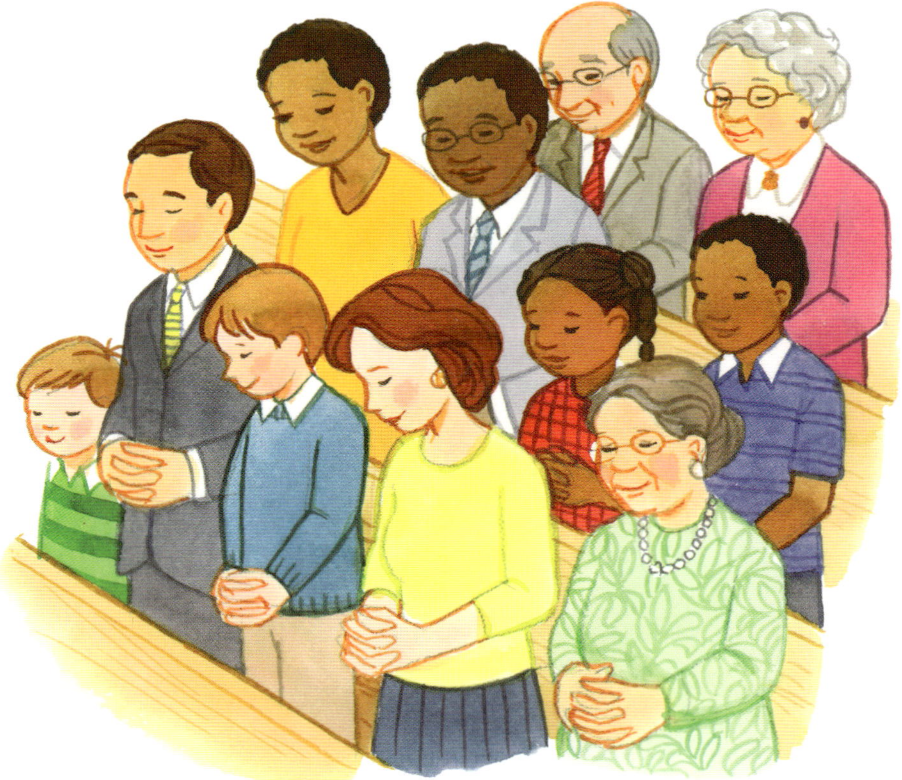

The organ is playing;

The bells chime along;

Hear the choir

Join in the song.

Action: *Pretend to play organ; pretend to ring bells.*

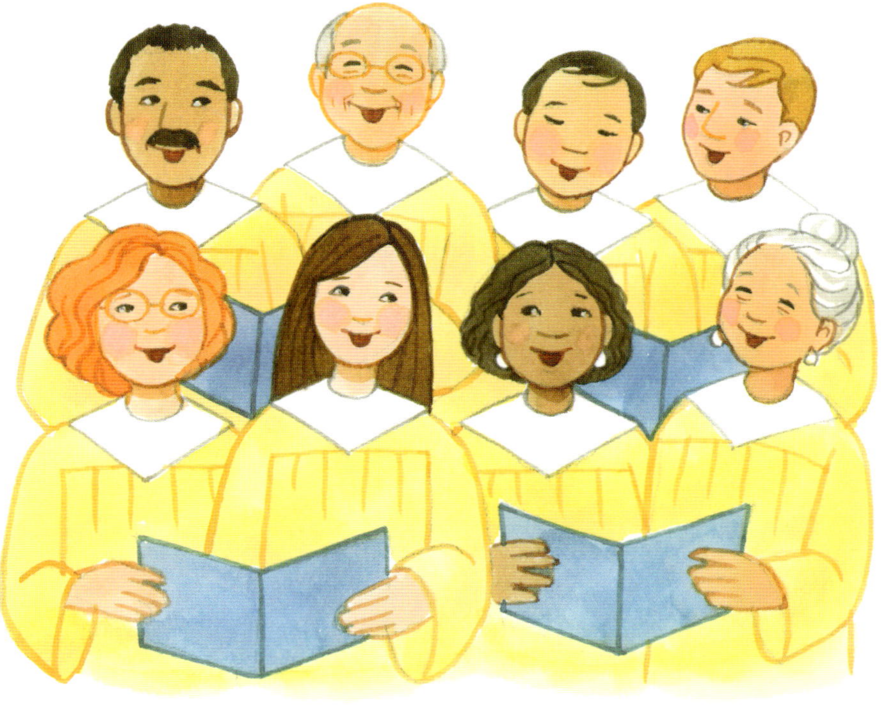

Here is the Bible.

From it we hear

That Jesus arose

And always is near.

Action: *Make closed book with hands; open hands.
Or put hands together to make an open book
and cup hands to ears.*

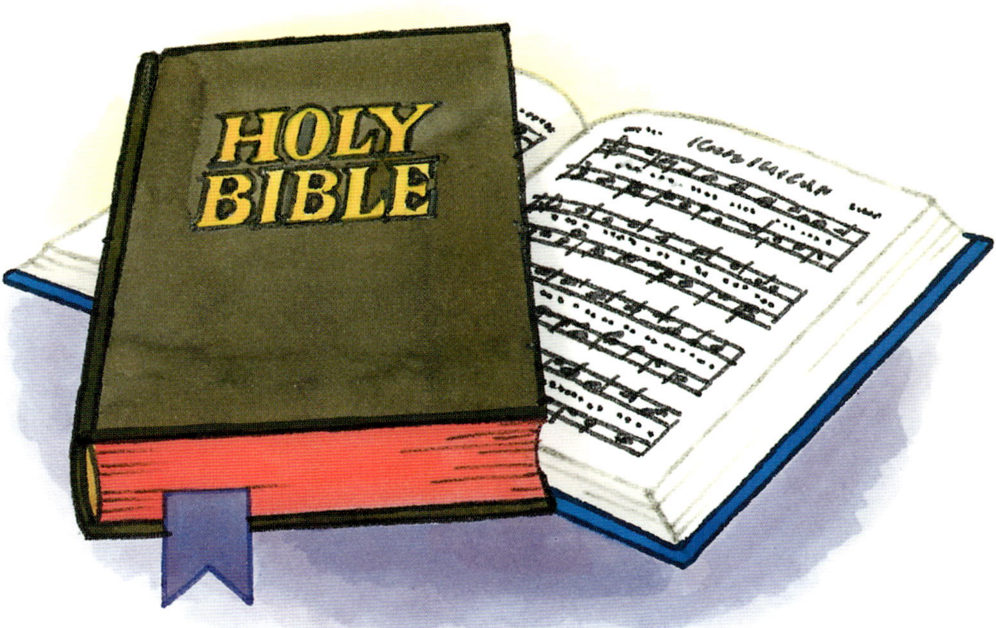
HOLY
BIBLE

Here is a cross.

Jesus, God's son,

Died on the cross

To save everyone.

Action: *Hold thumb and index fingers together to make a heart, then a circle. Make a cross with index fingers; then hold out hands for "everyone."*

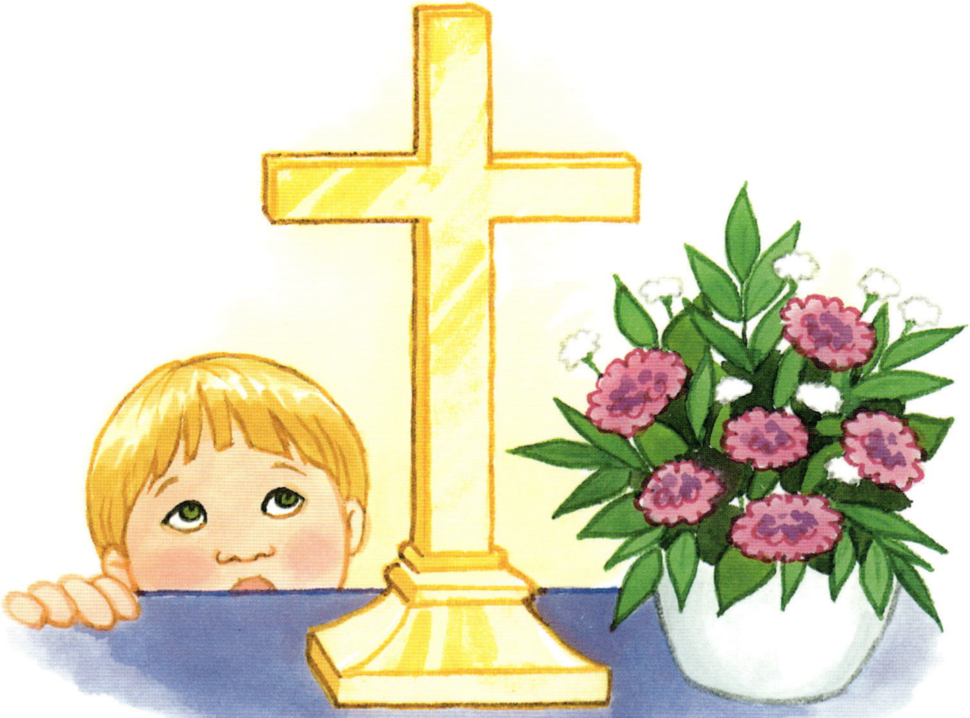

Open a hymnbook.

Happily raise

Unto the Lord

A glad song of praise.

Action: *Hold hands together to make an open book. Clap hands together on the word "praise."*

CONCORDIA COLLEGE LIBRARY
BRONXVILLE, NY 10708

Up in the pulpit,
The pastor will preach.
"Jesus loves children"
Is what he will teach.

Action: *Wrap hand around base of thumb on the other hand. Point upward with index finger.*

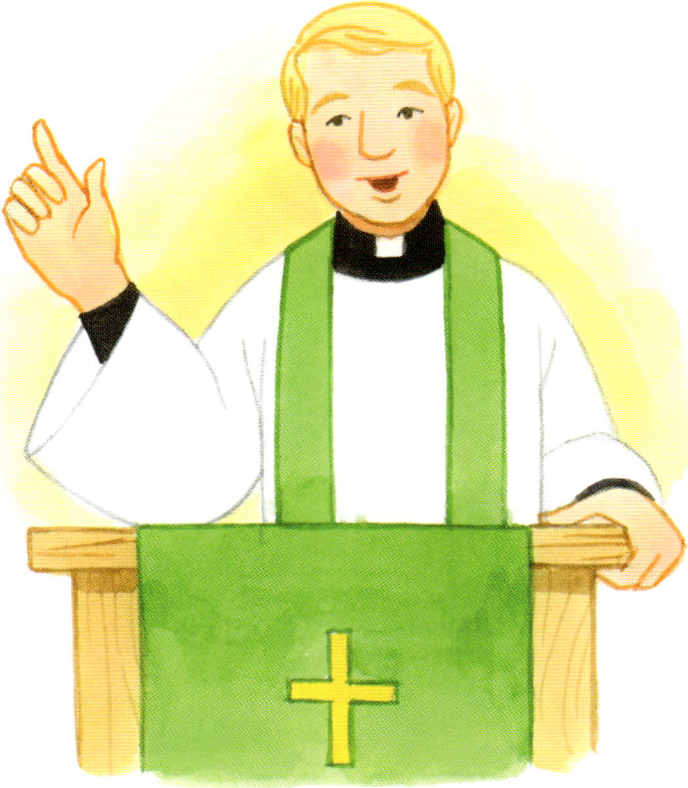

Do you see the font?

On our Baptism day,

God makes us His own,

Takes our sins away.

Action: *Cup hands together to make a bowl shape. Make sweeping motions with both hands for "away."*

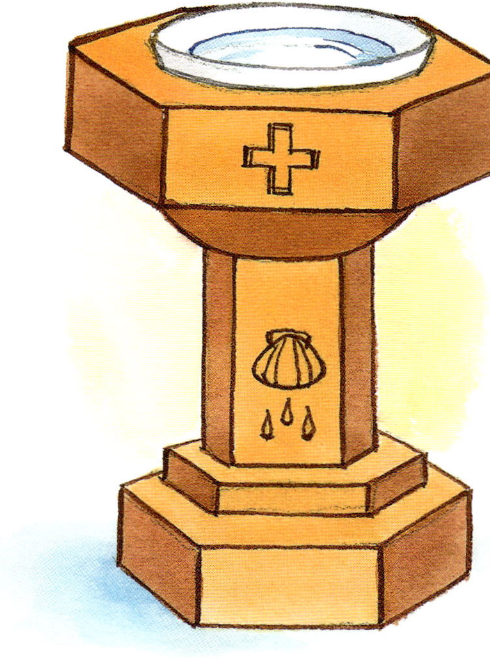

See on the altar

The wine and the bread.

Listen while words of

Forgiveness are said.

Action: *With palms inward, hold index fingers together to make altar; put thumbs up to make candles.*

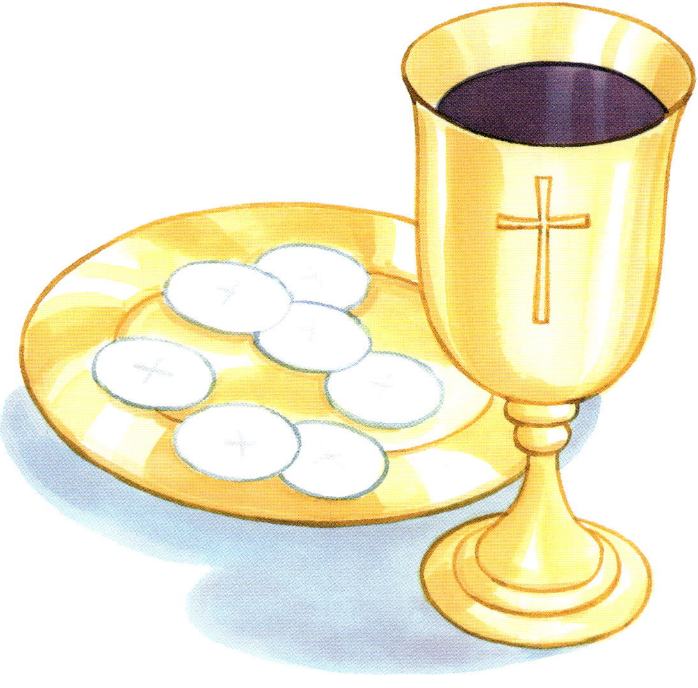

Time for the offering—
Put your gift in too
To thank God for blessings
He has given to you.

Action: *Pretend to give offering.*

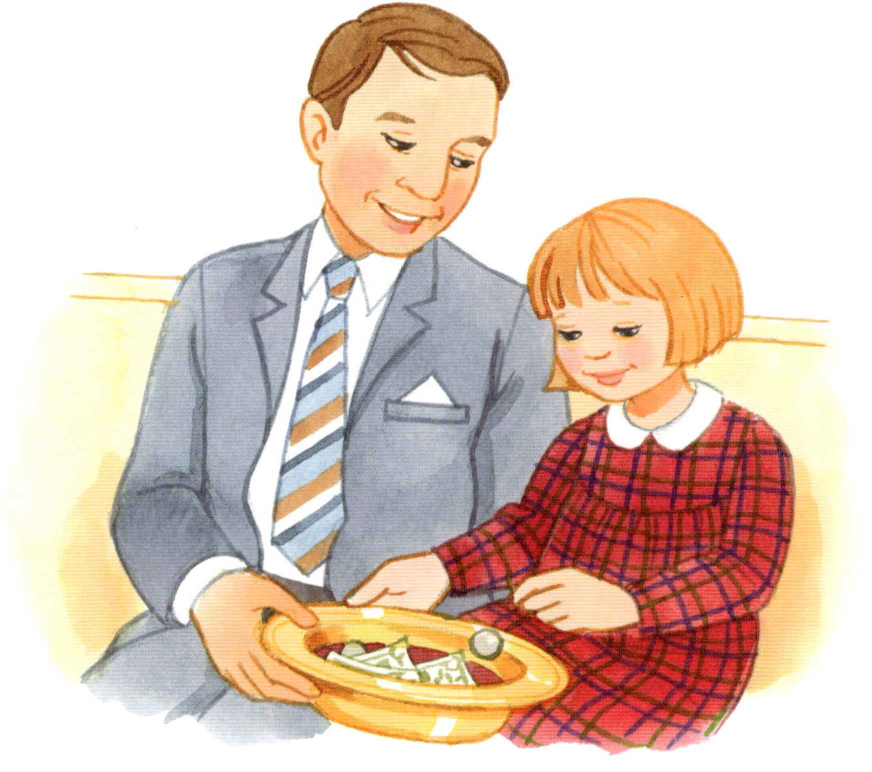

The service is over;
Now go on your way.
The Lord bless and keep you
In His peace today.

> **Action:** *Point to heaven; make cross with fingers.*

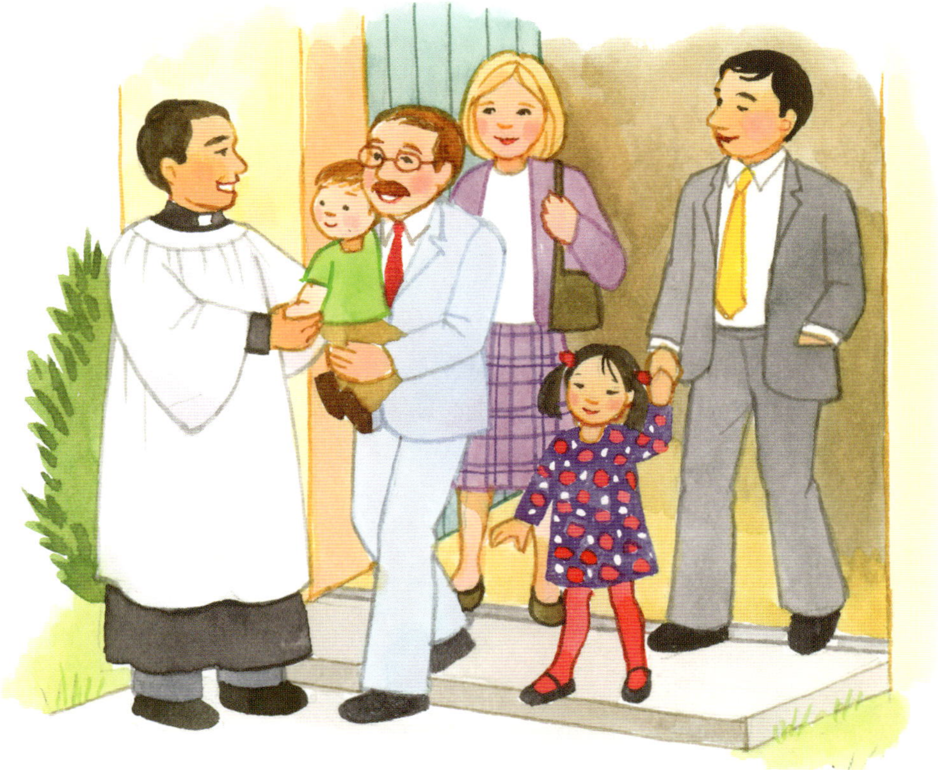

For Parents

Our Savior wants children of all times and places to come to Him, as we are reminded in Matthew 19:13–15 and elsewhere in the Gospels. We bring our little ones to Jesus when we go to church. There they hear God's love for them and join other children of God, old and young, in prayer, praise, and thanksgiving. Here are some suggestions for how you can encourage your child's understanding of what he or she sees and hears at church.

At church:
- Many churches reserve sections for young families, but some parents find that sitting toward the front helps young children be less distracted by people around them and have a better view of what goes on during the service.
- Encourage your child to participate in singing, praying, sharing the peace, giving an offering, going up for a children's sermon, receiving a blessing at the Communion rail, and other options your church provides.
- Bring along a "quiet bag" to use when short attention spans come to an end. In the bag, put quiet toys, such as a favorite stuffed animal, doodle or sketch toys, or other quiet things to play with. Include books and coloring books with a Christian theme.
- As your child learns to read, help him or her follow along in the hymnal or service folder.
- At a time when the sanctuary is empty, take your child to the chancel area to see the altar furnishings up close. Provide not just the names of what you see but also their meanings.

We bring our children to Jesus as we make our faith in Him a major component of our daily life. Here are suggestions for home activities to help you do so:

At home:

- Obtain a hymnal for use at home. Explain your church's order of worship and its meaning. Even if parts of your worship setting differ from examples given in this book, familiarizing your child with what he or she might see in other churches will make worship more meaningful.
- Make home devotions a part of your daily family life. As appropriate, Sunday readings and music can also be used in family worship. Follow an order of daily prayer or other order provided in your hymnal.
- Have your child help you set up a small altar for family worship, using a small table, dresser top, or cardboard box as a base. Help your child make simple objects such as a cross, banner, or candleholders to go with it. Together, decorate pieces of felt to make altar paraments that you can change with the Church Year.
- Make prayer a part of your family worship, using the Lord's Prayer and other appropriate church prayers as part of your family devotions.
- Encourage your child to do art projects with religious themes; then display them in your home. Make family art projects to use to decorate at Christmas or at other times during the Church Year.
- Sing to the Lord at home. Buy or make simple rhythm instruments for your child to accompany songs.
- Children who are taken to church often play church at home. Provide props, as appropriate, and see such play as a way in which your child is incorporating what he or she sees on Sunday morning into creative learning experiences. Early childhood church play may develop into grown-up church work as an acolyte, usher, reader, altar guild member, instrumentalist, or pastor.

Pray for God's guidance as you seek to raise your child as an active member of the one holy Christian Church of which we are all part.

To Him be glory in the church and in Christ Jesus